Healing in Limbo

A Book of Poetry

Carissa Lynn Taylor

PublishAmerica
Baltimore

ISBN: 978-1-4489-5492-6
PUBLISHED BY PUBLISHAMERICA, LLLP
www.publishamerica.com
Baltimore

Printed in the United States of America

*

This book is for some of my good friends and family.
To have one true friend is a blessing.
To have all of you in my life is a miracle!
I am sorry you did not make it into my last dedication,
However, I hope you know how much I love you:

Rose Arrigo, Shannon Brisbois, Angela Debella,
Brendan Gregory, Colin Gregory, Phillip Goralski,
Colin Hurley, Angela (Swiney) Jackson, David DeGuire,
Kristen (Rapplean) Mac, Barbara (Ocana) Mandrisch,
Amy (Ingham) Marcotte,
The May Family (Nik, Dan, Anissa, Daniel and Matthew),
Sera Rivers, Haley Stone, MaChelle Taylor,
Candis and Russell Thomeczek,
Kailee (Schmittlein) Warren and Heather Worsfold

To my wonderful father, *Harry E. Taylor Jr.,*
(I will always be your "Princess"),

In addition, to my amazing Godchildren:
Keith Webb, James Bakanosky
Taylor and Connor Hopkins,
Roman and Wyatt Poole,
And my lovely, lone girl…Hailey Thomeczek.
And to my honorary Godchildren: Shianne and Gabriel Poole.
"Auntie" loves you all so much!

To all my other friends and family—
You know who you are—
I will try to get you on the next one!

*

Always Near

I cannot believe it has been so long,
Almost ten years since you have been gone,
It is cruel that the world still goes on,
Without your shining smile.

How have we lived without you?
The time spent with you gone too soon.
I still hold you in my heart, the way the way the heavens hold the moon,
And your laughter lives on in my memory.

I know some grief will always last,
For you are part of my past,
And the empty space you left too vast,
To ever be refilled.

Deeply I carry my family with me,
They live on in the heart inside me,
And I am never lonely,
Because they, like you, are always near.

I believe the angels came and stole you,
Just to have the chance to know you,
Yet saved you more misery to go through,
And you can finally rest in peace.

To my Uncle, Richard Henry Warren
1956-1999
I miss you dearly, and will always love you!

Betrayal

From the time you were born,
You were special to me.
My cousin, like my own baby,
The bond between us so very strong.
As you grew and the whispers began,
I was there to quiet those wagging tongues.
When you were turned away from all others,
I welcomed you into my home,
Into my life.
After all, I loved you...

But you took my love,
The two of you,
And gave it to each other.
A secret, intimate exchange,
Of forbidden lust.
I was the last to know of the betrayal so grand,
And the humiliation like a weight crushing my heart.

From whom was the treachery the greatest?
In her...
My family,
The girl I had loved all of her life?
The one who shared the very blood in my veins,
And the memories in my head?
In him...
My husband,
The man who took a vow to love me forever?
The one whom I created my family with,
And believed would walk beside me in life?

I am better off now…
I am safe.
I have heard of true evil,
And I know it does exist.
For it lies in you—
The soul-less, heartless shells,
Pretending to be human.

But this…
This is my revenge,
My right to tell my story,
Where I am able to rid the anger and pain.

I expose the truth and darkness,
That is inside of you,
Here, where all the world can see,
And escape from your clutches,
Lest they be dragged as your companions,
To the deepest parts of hell,
Reserved for traitors of the heart.

Cosmic Gift

*

Round and round our world does turn.
No matter what our lives hold,
The cosmos continue to weave the web,
That is humanity.

*

When one is certain that life,
Cannot possibly deteriorate further,
We are put to yet another test,
A trial for our strength and faith.

*

When the world feels as solid as can be,
The bottom drops out,
And we find ourselves free falling without a net,
Wishing to the heavens, that we could fly.

*

But, sometimes, just sometimes,
When we least expect something wondrous,
Life sends the champion you needed,
A hand to hold when you are most alone.

*

In order to find this happiness,
You must reach the bottom first.
Only then can you know,
To hold on with all of your might,
And honestly appreciate
The cosmic gift that is love.

Deep, Dark Mystery

Don't give me your excuses,
I don't want your reasons why.
When we are all alone,
You seem to like me just fine.

You don't want anyone to know,
About our on-going affair,
Does being with me embarrass you?
Because, you say you do not care.

You come here everyday,
Kiss me every night,
You tell me when we make love,
It has never felt so right.

You won't touch me in public,
Can't wait to get me alone.
You hold me in your arms so tight,
When no one is around.

You call me, text me,
You know exactly who I am.
But, I won't be the deep, dark mystery,
You keep from all your friends.

Either you like me or you don't.
Please make up your mind.
Don't expect me to be there when you call,
Yet be the secret that you hide.

You've changed what I will accept,
From a relationship for the rest of my life,
But even for you I won't play these games.
It isn't worth my time.

Deepest Truth

Love has finally found me.
I hope it is here to stay.

In my wildest dreams,
I never knew it could feel this way.

Only when I am in your arms,
Do I find that place of perfect Zen.

I am lost each time you leave,
Until I am with you again.

These words come from my soul,
And are said with deepest truth.

Wherever you are, I will be,
You hold my heart as proof.

Depths of Fate

Danger is absolute.
I venture far,
Into the depths of fate.

As rational thought abandons me,
Numbness keeps calm,
My imprisoned soul.

Sorcery disguised as euphoria,
A ghastly tale unfolds.
Will insight ever return,
To enlighten me?

Don't Ask Me

Don't ask me to say, *"I love you"*
That wasn't part of the deal.
How can I find the words
For what I'm not supposed to feel?

Don't ask me to say, *"I miss you"*
When I turn and walk away.
We both knew this would happen,
Somewhere along the way.

Don't ask me to say, *"It kills me"*
To know someone else kisses your lips,
Or touches your sweet, soft skin,
With her fingertips.

Don't ask to say, *"I care"*
We agreed it would be this way,
That if we fell for each other,
One of us couldn't stay.

Don't ask me *"to remember"*,
The way you held me tight,
Sleeping soundly by your side,
Dreaming through the night.

Don't ask me, please, don't ask me this,
For then I can't deny,
All these deep, solid, feelings
For you, I have inside.

Fairy Tales

Where did you come from?
One day you just appeared,
Walked in through the mist,
All without warning.

I never saw it coming,
Like a spell has been cast,
By a fairy godmother.
I am enchanted by you,
As if by magic.

Illusion or Reality?
Dreaming or Awake?
I cannot believe my fortune,
This is too good to be true.
If I put on the glass slipper,
Will it fit?

Can we fly away,
On a magic carpet?
Build our castle,
In a beautiful kingdom?
It all seems possible,
With you.

My handsome Prince,
You are all the proof I need,
That fairy tales can come true.

Falling

What is this feeling,
That has come over me?
My stomach has dropped,
My head full of static,
Making me dizzy and disoriented.
The heat rises in my body,
Visibly making my face red and hot.
The air catches in my chest,
Making it hard to breathe.
I stumble along,
Trying to find my way,
With vision blurred.
I feel like I am falling.
Then suddenly I realize,
The cause is you,
And the way you make me feel.
It is I, frightened,
And fighting,
As I am falling in love.
I must let go,
And let my heart take over,
And simply take my solace,
In your arms.

For Gail

As sweet as can be,
It is impossible to dislike you,
Or to be anything,
Other than perfectly at ease with you.
I am honored to have you,
As my best friend.
As beautiful inside as out,
With an intelligence,
So many do envy.
You fit into my family,
As if you had been there,
All along.
We have been through so much,
Yet, we always knew,
We had each other.
You are another sister to me.
One who shares my secrets,
And too many "inside jokes" to count.
Having you in my life,
Makes me a better person,
Everyday.

For my best friend, Gail Ann (Forrester) Pedroza

For Hilary

Someone so young,
We are so many years apart,
Yet you are wise and strong,
And I learn from you everyday.
A wonderful person, spectacular mother,
You set the example,
The rest of us should follow.
Smart and funny,
Firm, but patient, and kind.
You never need to be asked,
You seem to instinctively know,
When a friend is in need,
And always come to the rescue.
Thank you for being my best friend,
Another sister to me.
You are truly,
A woman to be admired!

For my best friend, Hilary Justeen Loretta (Fought) Poole

For Maribeth

From the day we first met,
There was an inexplicable connection.
It was as if I had found,
The other half of me.
Those who know us,
Tease that we share a brain.
I believe it is a soul,
Divided into two bodies.
How else could we explain,
Knowing one another's thoughts
And feelings,
Without ever being told.
My best friend, another sister to me,
You live so far away.
Though we are never without each other,
I miss you always.
There is nothing about me
You do not know.
No secret left untold.
You are my friend,
My conscience,
My solid ground.
Without you I would be lost!

For my best friend, Maribeth Paige (Iavolo) Hopkins

Forever, Eternity

So far away,
Feels like forever,
Until again,
We will be together.

Weeks, and months, and years
Go by,
As we think of each other,
With tears in our eyes.

Our love for each other,
Grows stronger each day.
We know now,
We will always feel this way.

As we long for the time,
When it is just you and me,
And we can hold each other,
For all eternity.

Friends and Lovers

Is it not enough that I see you everyday,
That you are the only one in my life; in my bed?
Does it matter that I think you are wonderful,
And miss you when we are not together?
How can I begin to make you see,
How very much you mean to me?
Yes, Sweetheart, I like you, and love you as well,
Do I have to be *in* love with you too?
What if I cannot give that to you,
The way that you want me to?
Loving the way you kiss, the way you touch me,
The burning passion when we make love,
Does not mean I want to walk down the aisle,
Wearing a white dress, carrying a bouquet.
With you, I am completely at ease,
I would trust you with my very life,
But I will not take your name.
I have one of my own.
Can we just let this relationship be what it is,
Without wearing matching rings?
Friends and lovers, we are already committed.
Does that commitment require vows and a certificate
To make it real?
Please my dear, hold me tight, by all means,
But be careful not to crush me with your adoration.
I am afraid of heights, this pedestal much too tall.
I am just not ready to take the chance that I will fall.

Glorious Unity

Desire Awakens,
as Vivid Images
do Dance in Fluid Repetition
and Arrive Nebulous
in Calm Insistence
and Sensuality.
Dream Evaporates,
into Glorious Unity,
with Impatient Release
and Ecstasy.

Grow

My love for you,
Will always grow;
Like the waters of a river,
That do flow.

To hold you in my arms,
As you lay beside me,
Your love, like a blanket,
To protect and hide me.

To love you, hold you,
Cherish you forever,
And know in my heart,
We are eternally together.

Healing in Limbo

Forbidden love.
Forbidden touch.
They do not understand,
What brings us together.
All they have to do,
Is look, to really see.

When I am with you,
I can see the man,
You will become,
Though you are not completely there yet.

I know you truly see,
The woman that is me,
And respect all that I am,
Though life and experience,
Prevent full clarity.

If these years that separate us
Were only reversed,
Would we still be seen as unacceptable?
Or would our world,
Welcome us with open arms,
The way we do for each other?

Not a child,
But still so young,
Yet our souls connect,
And leave a trailing blaze of passion,
We cannot deny.

You were my friend,
Now a lover,
Based on a trust and closeness,
That has evaded us,
Until we put our fears aside,
And our faith in one another.

We are aware,
This is not everlasting,
But a short time spent in limbo,
Where we heal each other
And enjoy a happiness together,
If only for a little while.

Thank you my lover.
Thank you my friend.
You took me in broken,
And have made me whole again.
Though we must move on,
My heart is forever yours.

How Could You?

How could you go,
Without saying goodbye?

How could you not,
At least tell us why?

How could you hurt,
And not reach out for help?

How could you talk to us,
And never tell?

How could you just,
Give up one night?

How could you surrender,
And take your own life?

How could you think,
That was all you could do?

How could you not know
How much we loved you?

In loving memory of our dear friend,
Frank David Siegel

I Would Be Me

Co-written by: MaChelle Taylor

If I were sane, I would be free…
There would be no mental noise and obsession.
I would make good choices every time,
Without the need to over-think, stress myself out,
Or call people until I find the answers that I like best.
I would be confident in the decisions that I make.
I would consider God's direction,
As well as the consequences of my actions,
Because I would know
That the negative results,
Only compound to my obsessive thinking.

If I were sane, I would be free…
I would not have these conversations
Inside my own head.
I would not find pleasure,
In the pain of others.
I could not cause pain without remorse.
I would "give" without expecting,
Or being resentful.
I could love with my whole heart,
Not just the part of it that I can protect.
I would love openly and honestly.

If I were sane, I would be free…
I would let people see all of me.
I would understand myself,
And I would like who I am.
I would be able to trust,
Because I am trustworthy.

I would be able to love completely,
Because I love myself.
I could leave the past where it belongs,
In the past.
I could laugh with my whole soul.

If I were sane, I would be free...
I could listen,
Without my mind time traveling.
I would be able to truly relax,
Without fidgeting.
I could do the proper things,
Without different versions of right and wrong.
I would not second guess myself,
Or have to question my thoughts or actions.
I could enjoy today,
Because I am not thinking about tomorrow.

If I were sane, I would be free...
I would be comfortable alone,
Instead of just lonely.
I would not be confused,
I would have clarity of thinking.
I would not make excuses, deny or lie,
Because I would not need to.
I would not do things that are not necessary,
Cause myself harm, get anxious,
Or be consumed with self-pity.
I would have healthy relationships.

If I were sane, I would be free...
I would not be self-seeking.
I would stay in my own space,
And mind my own business,
Without having to constantly remind myself

To act properly.
I would not have to always justify
The decisions that are alone, mine.
I would be of sound mind.
Sanity would be God-like.
Resentments would be gone.

If I were sane, I would be free...
I would be happy, joyous, and released,
And know that I deserve it.
Sex could be ecstasy,
Because I could just feel,
Instead of thinking.
Fear would be gone.
Drama and emotional reacting would be minimized.
I would have no anger left.
I could clearly articulate what I feel.

If I were sane, I would be free...
I would be honest with myself,
As well as others.
I would be whole and complete,
The way I once was.
I would be confident,
Because I finally see what I am worth.
I would be ambitious,
Because I deserve to get ahead.
I would be healed,
I would be me.

I've Been Working on the Mustang

(For my son, Tristan: the car fanatic.
Sung to the tune of "I've Been Working on the Railroad")

I've been working on the mustang,
In the backyard all day.
I've been working on the mustang,
Getting her ready to race.
Can't you feel the sun a' shining,
While I'm changing the oil?
Can't you hear Mama calling,
"(Child's name)_____ don't beep that horn?"

(Child's name)_____ don't ya' beep,
(Child's name)_____ don't ya' beep,
(Child's name)_____ don't ya' beep that horn.
(Child's name)_____ don't ya' beep,
(Child's name)_____ don't ya' beep,
(Child's name)_____ don't ya' beep that horn.

(Child's friend, sibling, etc. name) _____ is in the yard with (child's
name) _____,
(Another of child's friend, sibling, etc. name) ___ is in the yard also…
(Another of Child's friend, sibling, etc. name) _____ in the yard with
(child's name) _____,
Cranking up the radio!

Be bop bidly bop oh,
Be bop bidly bop ohhhhh,
Be bop bidly bop oh,
Crankin' up the radio!

Journey Long...

Can you believe, my friend,
How things have changed?
Oddly enough,
Our lives have run much the same.

What we have been through,
So very much,
On each other we leaned,
When times have been tough.

New places, our returned names,
We packed up our children,
Decided no more games.

But, this new road,
You are traveling home,
Is where I cannot go,
You must walk it alone.

Please remember, my friend
Though your journey is long,
At the end I will stand,
Still cheering you on.

Always a Taylor girl, "MaC",
One day at a time...

Leap of Faith

In life there are very few certainties.
Everyone will tell you the only sure things,
Are death and taxes,
But to truly live life to the fullest,
One must at some point in their existence,
Take a plunge into the unknown.
An abyss that has yet to be explored.
You must close your eyes,
Take a deep breath,
And jump with both feet,
Into the darkness.
No one can guarantee a soft landing.
You have to take the chance,
That the chasm could be harmful,
even fatal
But, if you had the courage to try,
The daring to test the unimaginable.
If the bottom is rough,
And there was nothing to catch you,
And need to fight for survival,
Until you can move on,
Knowing and understanding,
That though you fell,
You will keep this knowledge forever.
Sometimes, if we are fortunate,
We land on a soft bed of roses,
And walk away unscathed,
But with a new valor,
You were never aware of,
And the treasure more glorious,
Because you earned it…
By taking,
That Leap of Faith.

Let Me Call You Sweetheart

"She is such a doll,
So sweet, so nice."
This is all correct,
Unless you cross her twice.

The first time it happens,
She will politely forgive your sin,
But the next time,
It will get right under her skin.

When "Little Miss Sweet"
Starts to feel that itch,
She makes the transformation,
Into "Incredible Bitch!"

She really is a good person,
So very smart, so very strong,
But her personal motto:
"I will not be walked upon!"

If you want to be her friend,
You had better know this part…
Make sure you never, ever screw
With that nice "Sweetheart!"

Life of the Party

Two words to describe you?
Hmmm…let me see,
I would say *"Hot Shit"*,
All too easily!

Your card games,
And dirty jokes,
You picking up those "French boys",
With fries and a coke.

Vacations at Old Orchard,
Are not the same without you,
Karaoke night is less fun,
That is sure true!

So full of life,
So very much fun,
In your 80's still ready to party,
Or just relax with a "cold one."

We miss you terribly,
In our memories you live on,
Always smiling and laughing,
Always so strong!

In Loving Memory of our Aunt,
Simone I. (Rivard) Hunkins
1923-2006

A Little Fun

I like you very much,
I love you even more.
You are quite easily,
A man I could adore.

Please, my dear,
Remember this is a "fling".
I am not in love with you,
It is not the real thing.

Infatuation, pleasure?
Most definitely, yes!
Passion and attraction,
At its very best!

I wish so much,
I could offer you more.
But, marriage, commitment?
You are knocking on the wrong door.

I have been scorched, and burned,
I need to be free.
Just because I want you,
Does not mean it must be.

For now, just to be able to trust,
And have a little fun,
I chose you, my friend,
To be that someone.

If in love I ever fall,
Deeply and true,
And I have my choice...
It would have to be you!

Living Ghost

Go haunt someone else's life...
Rattle your chains in their attack.
What proof have you given us,
That you should even matter.

Don't want your voice in our ears,
Your footsteps on our floor.
You are a spirit long ago mourned,
Knock on another door.

A living ghost we have exorcised,
Though you still walk the Earth.
Your credit here has expired,
And us...you don't deserve.

You've made your choice...as have we,
Now please walk towards the light.
You are out of time, out of chances,
Your existence cannot be called a life.

We are free and at peace,
No ghosts are welcome here.
Carry your shackles somewhere else,
You have no power here!

Long Walk

On a rainy, Spring morning,
He took my hand and we began our journey.
The sun soon replaced the rain and it was beautiful.
Somewhere along the way it began to grow dark.
Occasionally we would step out of the shadows,
And I would see him clearly, there beside me.
Those bright spaces soon disappeared completely,
As did he.
I could not feel him, I could not see him.
There was only dark.
The gloom so thick I could feel it wrapped around me,
Like a big, woolen blanket.
I stopped.
There I stayed, huddled in fear for what seemed an eternity.
A voice that came from down inside me asked,
"Who is this pitiful creature hiding here,
Waiting to be rescued by him?"
I was astonished. Certainly it was not me!
When had I changed so much?
I realized I must continue walking
In order to find the light and my freedom.
The road was long, it was rough, it was difficult.
I was tired.
I pushed on, I could not give in.
I had to fight, had to persevere!
And, there it was…
An opening in the dark, and a world so bright,
I feared I would be blinded.
I ran to it with all the strength I had left.
And then…I was home.
I had been so absorbed by him and his will,

I never noticed the cave I had wandered into,
Until it was too late, and I was lost.
But that cave had an opening.
It was the long way home, and well hidden,
But I found it,
And an inner strength I had forgotten was mine.
He never came for me, never even looked back.
It no longer mattered.
I lost him, and found me,
And a happiness I never knew was possible.

Metamorphosis

A soul in despair,
As low as she can be,
Like a caterpillar crawling,
Across the ground on her belly.
She moves slowly,
Alone and afraid.
Waiting for the next footfall
To step down and crush her,
Leaving her broken and gone.

She makes it safely to the tree,
Tired she wonders:
Should she climb or lie down,
And give up the battle?
The branch is so high,
And she is overwhelmed by exhaustion.

Self-preservation takes control,
She pushes herself higher,
Until the destination is reached.
Ready for a long, peaceful rest,
She wraps herself in a protective cocoon.

During her long sleep,
She decided to make a change.
She would become strong,
Independent, a new look on life.
After all,
She has made it this far,
On her own.

One lovely day,
The cocoon opens,
Instead of the frightened caterpillar,
Crawling on her belly,
A new her emerges:
A grand butterfly,
Ready to take flight,
With beautiful new wings.

Photo Courtesy of Carissa Taylor © 1987

My Uncle, Richard Henry Warren

Photo Courtesy of Gail Pedroza © 2008

My best friend, Gail Ann (Forrester) Pedroza

My best friend, Hilary Justeen Loretta (Fought) Poole

Photo Courtesy of Lindsey Taylor © 1997

My best friend, Maribeth Paige (Iavolo) Hopkins

Photo Courtesy of Cheryl Olson © 1999

Frank David Siegel

Photo courtesy of Hilary Poole © 2008

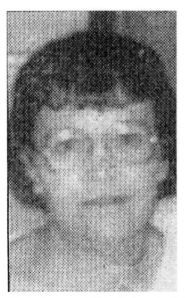

Simone I. (Rivard) Hunkins
1923-2006

Photo Courtesy of Claire Bakanosky © 2004

Carissa Taylor

Photograph 2008 © Lindsey Taylor

Photo Courtesy of Carissa Taylor © 2006

My exquisite Mother,
Cheryl Lois (Cantara) Olson

More Q and A

"The only sure things in life, are death and taxes."?
Thank you. You have made me feel sooo much better.
No wonder depression is on the rise!

"I can't help falling in love with you."?
Duh! That's why it's called "falling" in love.
Otherwise it would be "leaping" or something else corny like that!

"You're shitting me"?
You know what? I have never quite understood how this became a
popular phrase. Does it make sense to anyone else?

"Who let the dogs out?"
Seriously? This is the best you could come up with?
Who cares? Get off your lazy ass, and bring them back in.

"Cut off your nose to spite your face"?
Sounds pretty serious! I say if you are dumb enough to do this,
Then you deserve what you get!

"Life is like a box of chocolates, you never know what you're gonna get"?
Well, the good chocolates have a diagram to tell you exactly which one
you are getting.

"Why do you build me up, Buttercup?"
Maybe because you insist on calling me these stupid pet names…
Just a thought, leave names like this for plant life, where they belong.

"Crack of dawn"?
I don't know about you, but at my house, dawn comes as a blinding light
that drags my tired ass out of bed!

"As they say"?
Who is they exactly? Has anyone actually figured this out yet?

"Come on Baby, light my fire"?
Newsflash!!! This may have worked for Jim Morrison, but you just sound like an idiot when you say it.

"It could happen"?
Ummm, probably not. This is one of those things said to make other people feel better. I say let them face the rejection now instead of later!

"Pleased to meet you. Hope you guessed my name"?
Why do I have to guess? Can't you just get on with it and tell me?

"Life goes on"?
Wow, and I thought I was the only one on the planet. Thanks for clearing that up for me!

"Can I eat that"?
Logic should tell you that if you have to ask if it is edible, you should probably leave it alone.

"The best things in life are free"?
I would be inclined to agree, if I didn't already know that this is crap! When was the last time you knew this statement to be true?

"Stupid is as stupid does"?
The key word here is "stupid", why are you still trying to make sense of it?
Stop wasting time and move on!

"There is someone for everyone"?
Ok, hate to burst your bubble here, but some people just suck.
Good luck finding someone to put up with their issues.

"Why"?
Oh shut up! I've heard that question enough from my toddler. You're supposed to be a grown-up, figure it out!!!

"Did you have a good day at work"?
Dude, I was at work. How good could it have been, really?

"Nice guys finish last"?
No, slow guys finish last. Hurry your ass up!

"Frailty, thy name is woman"?
My response: childbirth. Let's see a man try that!

"Imagination is more important than knowledge"?
Too much imagination could get you a lovely padded cell at Belleview.

"At the touch of love, everyone becomes a poet"?
Or a stark-raving lunatic too blind to find their way out of a paper bag!

"Goodnight, Sweet Prince"?
I usually just say, "shut up and go to sleep", but if you find a true "prince", Give him my number!

"Management is doing things right, leadership is doing the right things"?
Three words for you: George W. Bush
(Need I say more?)

"I don't think. I know!"?
I don't think you know either!

Mother's Love

A child cannot fathom the love their mother feels,
Until they in turn have a child of their own.
The way the entire world changes,
In the blink of an eye,
When it is realized that a new life,
A beautiful, new life, that you created,
Is growing inside your body.

How sweet it is to feel those little legs kicking,
Watching the screen as you suck your thumb,
And move around the home that will hold you,
Until you are ready to meet the world,
And me.

A son will never know the extent of his mother's love.
He will never hold in his arms,
The baby that has been part of you for so long,
That you already know and love,
But have yet to gaze upon.

A daughter will one day understand that bond,
When she receives the miracle that is becoming a mother.
A son can love his child,
And protect with a fierceness he has never known,
But will not take part in the transformation into motherhood.

My boy, as your mother,
All I can do is my best to bestow upon you
The understanding that will make you,
The greatest man, husband, and father you can be.
That is my gift to you,

To prepare you for the world ahead,
And tell you that all I am now,
Is because I became your mother.

My Boy

I remember so well,
The day you were born.
I held you in my arms,
Our special bond was formed.

I look at you now,
And I cannot believe,
That baby boy,
Is the young man I now see.

From changing diapers,
To patching scraped knees,
"The Big Bad Wolf"
And me, yelling "Get out of that tree!"

The kisses and hugs,
Going out to play,
Coaxing you into nap time,
Picnics during the day.

Watching you skateboard,
Watching you roller skate,
Seeing you play baseball,
Letting you stay up late!

So many things,
We have been through together,
I the proud Mother,
Could go on forever…

No matter how old,
Or how tall you are,
You will always be my sweet boy,
So special to my heart!

For My Godson, Keith Allen Webb.

My Dreams

Every night,
While I'm asleep,
I feel your arms,
Tight around me.

Each morning, I awake,
And you aren't there,
It gives a feeling,
Of deep despair.

Until you are mine,
I am happiest in my dreams,
I long to stay there,
And never leave.

I hope when I am with you,
It does blatantly show,
For I love you,
I hope that you know.

For now I have my dreams,
Maybe someday they will be true,
And when I awake,
I will be looking at you.

No, I Do Not Mind

No, I do not mind the early mornings,
Or the clutter of all the toys,
All those Disney toddler shows,
The seemingly endless noise.
I wake each day at the crack of dawn,
To a smile, "Hi Mama" and a kiss.
It is hard to have a bad day,
When it begins like this.

No, I do not mind the tiny fingerprints,
On the window glass,
Or the funny things he says,
That really make me laugh.
From a scene in "Herbie",
He repeats, "You want a piece of me?"
Not sure why that stuck with him,
But it's as cute as it can be.

No, I do not mind the messiness,
That comes with every meal,
Or the sweet pout he gives,
When he does not want that apple peeled.
He tries so hard to help me out,
With all my daytime chores,
But his most favorite part,
Is when I vacuum all the floors!

No, I do not mind this full-time job,
Though a lot of work it is,
But more than that is all the fun,
Of playing like a kid.

No matter how old he is,
Or where he chooses to go,
The best part of my life is spent with him,
My little boy, I love him so!

For my sweet, wonderful boy:
Tristan Cary.
My life is all I could ever hope for,
Because I have you!

Not with You

We started out friends,
We hoped for more,
And here I am,
Lying in your arms today…

I never wanted this feeling to end,
But life has a way,
Of opening new doors,
And I know,
You have to go away…

I was not supposed to fall in love,
Not with you.
I knew it was exactly what I could not do,
Not with you!

Now you are leaving,
All I can do is watch,
And pray,
For you to hold me,
And forever stay…

I have these feelings,
I cannot hide,
I never knew
You would be the one,
And now I cannot let you go…

As you hold me,
Through this last night,
I hope morning,

Will not come,
Because it is you,
The only one I love…

Every moment with you,
I will remember,
I wish so very much,
I could hold you always.

Maybe, someday,
We can be together,
Again,
Without seeing an end in sight.

Old Flames of Love

From each of you, I learned
How to love a little more,
How to fall,
How to go on…

Were we really so young?
Brendan, my first love, still my friend,
Who lit the fire,
That would someday make my passion burn.

The end of childhood, we knew it all.
Mark, we grew up, and grew apart,
Yet taught each other so much.

My best friend, I could not see you,
Nathan, until it was too late.
The lost love I had not realized in time,
And would never have the chance to go back.

You were so sweet.
Brian, we were becoming
Who we were meant to be.
We fell in love at rest stop of life,
Before we went our separate ways.

Despite all odds,
Ryan, with you I took a chance,
And learned that even though it failed,
In the nightmare that was us,
I was blessed with my children,
The greatest gift of all

When life had me broken,
David, you showed me
How to live again,
To be a woman with my head held high.

One Night

From the day we met,
I never thought I would forget,
What it was like,
To hear your voice on the phone,
Or all those late nights,
Spent driving you home.

Then one day,
You moved away.
I knew I could not,
get you to stay.
As a best friend,
All I could say,
Was "Goodbye"!

But, I got older,
And I grew,
I also moved away,
And, still ended up near you.

Once again,
We talked on the phone,
About enjoying our lives,
All on our own.

One night you came,
To visit me,
And something happened,
I could not foresee…

That special friendship,
Between you and me,
Took a turn,
And formed something new.

All of a sudden,
I wanted much more,
Than this friendship,
I had so long adored.

I felt strange,
Saw something different in you,
That is when I finally knew,
Somehow during this friendship,
I fell in love.

I believe the old saying goes,
"What lays ahead, nobody knows."
So here I am,
Alone again,
Without the one I love,
Without my best friend.

To someone else,
He belongs,
But as they say,
"Life goes on."

I still cannot help,
But to ask inside,
"If I had spoken sooner,
Would he be mine?"

"There is someone,
For everyone."
As someone else,
Will always say.

Maybe, just maybe
I will find you again,
Somehow,
Someday!

For my lost friend from long ago...
You know who you are...
We'll always have "Memphis."

One Who Got Away

It used to be us.
Always you and I,
We seemed inseparable.
We had each other, my friend,
And our world was complete.

Those nights we stayed up,
Talking until morning,
About nothing, about everything.
Singing old songs,
While you played your guitar.

All of those wonderful moments,
Spent together,
And yet we never said,
How we really felt.
Never knowing you would become,
The One Who Got Away.

One beautiful night,
Completely unexpected or forgettable,
Holding each other,
Expressing our feelings,
With kisses instead of words.
It was an innocent night,
Though I wish it had not been.

It was you all along,
The one I wanted,
The one I pushed away,
When you got too close,

Sending you straight
Into someone else's arms.
Making you become
The One Who Got Away.

Not a word spoken,
We lost one another,
And our precious friendship.
Five years of wondering,
How I could have been so very blind.

Then you returned,
A ghost ship drifting,
Appearing through the mist.
My anger and broken heart preventing,
What could be a second chance.
But again I allowed you to become,
The One Who Got Away.

My path has ended,
And I stand alone.
Still dreaming, still missing,
Still wishing,
It was me beside you.
Still hurting from this hole in my heart,
Where you used to be.

If I could go back,
You would be my change.
I would stand tall,
I would tell of my love for you,
And make sure you would never become,
The One Who Got Away.

Package Deal

You say that you want me.
Are you completely sure?
I do not come alone…
To me there is so much more…

I am a package deal,
Though without ribbons or bows.
Just a special gift from Heaven,
That makes my whole world glow.

It is not dessert or candy,
Or any kind of treat.
What I have in my life,
Is a thousand times as sweet!

Not a trip or vacation,
But everyday is an adventure.
No, not a pet either…
Though some days I have to wonder!

Decorations? Still not even close,
But my home is incomplete without it.
No, not new clothes either…
Though I often have remnants on my outfit!

Not a new truck or car,
But can occasionally *drive* me crazy.
Not a movie in a theatre,
Though the plot is quite amazing!

His laughter is music to my ears.
He is a blessing from God to take care.
If you can make the commitment,
My dream I am willing to share.

Your love must be unconditional,
Regardless of what may happen.
For when the day ends,
It is my son that really matters.

Yes, he is the package part of the deal,
My sweet, little boy.
The constant reason that my life,
Is filled with so much joy!

Precious, Little Cry

Shivering and cold all over,
No sign of any warmth.
I only want to hear the cry,
Of the child that I have born.

I feel my life-blood flowing,
I know it will soon be time,
I want to stay long enough,
To see this child of mine.

The only noise I hear,
Is a constant droning hum,
Why won't my baby cry?
Please, I need to hear it once.

Darkness is setting in now,
I have a single wish,
To hold my healthy child,
And give him just one kiss.

The shaking and the cold have stopped,
The pain no longer there.
Tell me that my son is alright,
All else I do not care.

All of a sudden, there it is,
That sweet, beloved sound...
The tiny, precious, little cry,
And again to my Earthly body I am bound.

I have been returned from the hands of death,
Knocking loudly upon my door.
All it took was one small, sound,
From my baby boy!

Sacrifice

For someone so young,
You are wise beyond your years.
All around you,
The people in your life,
Look to you for answers.
They know,
With all you have,
You will protect them,
Even at your own sacrifice.

You give them freedom,
They hold you captive.
You are bound to them,
By the blood in your veins.
Though you dream of escape,
You are aware
They will never willingly,
Let you go.

You believe you find peace,
Here in my arms.
You cannot linger here,
For I do not hold
What you honestly seek.
If you were to remain,
It would be a life of love,
Yet a prisoner you would still be,
As our hopes and dreams,
Are not the same.

Not a boy, still very youthful,
You must find your own path,
You must stand tall
And build what you have long desired.
You must release
Those that hold you too dear,
So they may realize,
Their own strengths
And find their own adventures.

I must release you
To see that you succeed.
For if I truly cherish you,
I must set you free,
To mature into the man,
That fate has destined you to become,
And at long last,
Live in that peaceful world,
You so deserve.

Sink or Swim

I was a child,
Most of you were grown.
Here I am a woman,
With children of my own.

What happened to our clan,
Our big, fun-loving team?
Many of you have turned,
So cruel and so mean.

Hardened in life,
Bitter as well.
Some are downright evil,
Come straight out of Hell!

We all make bad choices,
To be human is to err.
We need to learn from our mistakes,
Believe me, I have my share.

I will not throw my arms up,
Give in because I am down.
Life is sink or swim,
And I will not drown!

We were so close,
Now we are miles apart.
I have decided here,
To make a new start.

I love you all,
And still hold you dear,
But I keep *my* family away,
Your negativity I fear.

You do not hold you life,
With any esteem,
And I will not allow those who are jaded
To shatter our dreams.

Sleeping Prisoner

I used to be independent. I used to be strong.
I used to be confident.
I had so many goals, wishes, hopes, and dreams.
Then I met him…

I cannot be sure where I went, or who I was.
Those goals, wishes, hopes, and dreams,
Faded into his world…

Imprisoned, sedated inside my body,
Another person looking through my eyes,
Speaking with my lips,
While the real me slept inside my cell.
Awakening seldom,
Only to pound on the door for my freedom,
Until my energy was lost, and asleep again I fell,
With exhaustion.

But he became too self-assured, too bold, too arrogant,
And turned careless.
Why waste his time locking the gate?
After all, "Sleeping Beauty" never truly rises,
Without true love's kiss.
And, he knew that was not him—
My warden.

But, life is not a fairy tale,
And I am no Princess!
I was able to walk away without his help,
Or permission,
Because I do not need it.

It did not take long for "me" to awaken,
And take back what was rightfully mine—
My life.

My strength, confidence,
and independence, have taken a beating.
But, they are healing.
My goal, wishes, hopes and dreams,
Have all become memories…
But I can let them go,
Without shedding tears,
Because new ones have taken their place.

I have a lot of work to do
And I am afraid.
But, I can do this and be successful.
After all, I have faced worse—
I have faced him—
And set myself free!

Sociopath

Be very careful ladies…
The Big Bad wolf is out tonight.
He is not the nightmare you picture,
Just the handsome "Mr. Right."

He will observe you closely,
Before he begins whispering his lies into your ear.
He is a quick study, honey,
He knows exactly what you wish to hear.

Before you know it, the trap is set,
Through the door you walk right in.
This will not bother his conscience,
There is no consequence for his sins.

While he bleeds you dry and steals your life,
He is lining his next victim up.
The cons are smooth from all his practice,
He never plans to stop.

He will stay until you are a shell,
Of the woman which you used to be.
When he has used you up, he will toss you away,
And move on so happily.

Beware all you innocents,
For this matter is not for laughs,
It is difficult to look through the "Dream Guy"
And spot the real Sociopath!

Tamed Hearts

It seems like we have been friends forever.
Everyone thought we would be together.

Inside,
We secretly felt the same.
Towards each other,
We kept our hearts tamed.

Then With you,
That one precious night,
When we shared that perfect kiss,
and I saw the light.

Asleep I fell,
Wrapped in your arms,
Knowing with you,
I would be safe from harm.

Another person
In your life,
Does complicate,
what could be so right.

Who would have thought,
We would come to this?
After what supposed to be,
An innocent kiss.

Thank You

You were so young,
Lost in a world with few chances,
Alone even in marriage.
But, you are a force of life,
This world could not contain,
Or reckon with.

So wise, so driven,
You have never stopped trying,
To better yourself, your life,
As well as us and ours.

I have learned so much from you,
You with the voice of an angel,
My friend, my teacher…
My Mother.

I thank you.
I love you!

To my exquisite Mother,
Cheryl Lois (Cantara) Olson

Toddler Dictionary

As any parent can tell you, it is not uncommon for a toddler to speak in a language entirely of their own creation. Here are some words that my son has come up with. Not only did they have me laughing…but, also took me forever to figure out what they meant! Hope you enjoy them as much as I did.

A fine oh in—Find another one
A-Pee—Grampi
Ah pain—Airplane

Baby (or Good boy)—all humans fit into one of these categories
Boatsnaggin'—Volkswagen
Bot-a-appah—Bite an apple
Buh Yow—Bottle
Bye-a-fy—Butterfly

Ca-yah-pee-yah—Caterpillar
Can-nip-ma—Camera

Dees win—This one
Doggie—All mammals with the exclusion of humans and whales
Duck sigh—Dark outside
Duh-wink—Drink
Duss-yu-me—Just you and me

Fassnight—Flashlight
Fi-Yah—Flower
Funtas-sick—Fantastic

Ga-oh-dare-Go over there

Ha-tear—Highchair
Huppy-cah—Herbie car
Hut—Heart

Is mason—Imagination

Ken-fine-deet—Can't find it

Me-sun—Nissan
Mo-yah-psycho—Motorcycle

Nano-tips—Potato chips
Napshake—Lampshade
New pucking—No parking
Nigh-ning—Lightning
No Kay—No, I do not want to do that
Noop—Snooze
Not cuss—Nutcase
Nut-yoose—It's not yours

Pass-set-bowl—Basketball
Pay talk—Play with chalk
Pay-gwon—Playground
Pew-yah—Computer
Piece-cah—Police car
Puncape—Pancake (also applies to cupcake)

Sa-yee—Sally (big fan of Disney's Cars)
Stinky-bow—Tinkerbell

Tickin-flies—Chicken and fries
Tub-beeson-uf—Television off
Two a bus—Toothbrush

Um-oken—I'm looking (also cooking)
Um-pissed—Impressed
Up-a-not—Astronaut

Yid-um-pine—Little Einsteins
Yigh-un-keen—Lion King
Youkit-a-mall—Look at them all
Yuh-you—I love you

Truth

Why do we waste so much time
Using words we do not need
Instead of honestly sharing
The feelings we have?
Why can I not look at you
And tell you what is in my heart?

I have a million butterflies in my stomach
Each time you gaze into my eyes.
When you hold me,
I feel like I could walk through fire,
As long as I am close to you.
You take my breath away
With your sweet kisses.
My world disappears
When we make love.

Why do we waste so much time
Using words we do not need
Instead of honestly sharing
The feelings we do have?
Why can I not look at you
And tell you what is in my heart?

You are my friend, my confidant,
My shoulder to cry on, the one I share my victories with,
I can tell you anything,
And I am truly myself with you.
Yet the most important words,
I cannot bring myself to speak to you.
What I need to say, goes unsaid,

The feeling of being complete escaping me,
With those three missing words...
The final piece of the puzzle
That is my very core.

Why do we waste so much time
Using words we do not need
Instead of honestly sharing
The feelings we do have?
Why can I not look at you
And tell you what is in my heart?

How do I put my fear aside?
The fear that you will not return my affections,
When I finally whisper the truth...
That you have defied my every expectation,
Moved me in ways I could never have imagined,
And that I have fallen
Totally and completely
In love with you.

25 Things to Know About Men

(co-written by: Michael Brueckmann, David DeGuire, Phillip Goralski and Jim Lambright)

1. They have only four major needs for survival: Sex, alcohol, sleep and food

2. Yes, they think about sex all the time. This is common knowledge, not a secret. Get over it!

3. Sex with someone else is roughly like being alone, except that the other person helps with the work.

4. On the same note, don't threaten them with sex. It's kind of like video games, they are fun with other people, but can be played alone.

5. Despite the rumors, men do not give the kind of details that women do. Theirs are more like "Hey, did you do it?"

6. If they are feeling really feisty, they may ask "Was it good?"

7. Most men want a woman who can be a lady in public and a whore in the bedroom. Ladies, you already know this. You don't have to like it. You don't even have to do it, but don't pretend otherwise.

8. Maxim magazine is *Cosmo* for men. Seriously, try reading it sometime! They know it too, they just don't want to be reminded.

9. Yes, they look at beautiful women whom they see in public. They are not blind, neither are you. Come on chickie, you saw her too! He doesn't get pissed when you drool over Brad Pitt on TV. Let's face it, there is about the same chance. Again, they know this too...

10. No, pregnant women don't bother them. The belly is irrelevant, because they are focused on the bigger boobs!

11. Chick flicks make they want to slip into a temporary coma. They are just not programmed to find that shit interesting.

12. Men don't cry at movies, because they are MOVIES!!!

13. If it has explosions, sex, and death in it, they like it. End of story. Remember this when picking out a movie for date night.

14. Don't pretend you didn't already know that. This just irritates the living shit out of them!

15. They do not have a clue what is fashionable. They do not care. So, quit asking about your clothes.

16. They do not necessarily hate to shop. They just hate to shop for your stuff.

17. If you are going to ask about "girlie stuff" (i.e.: shoes, makeup, hair, etc.) then you need to give a clue what you want to hear. Preferably the answer that will best get them laid later!

18. Same as with us, if he did not ask your opinion on his choice of attire, it is because he does not want it. He likes what he picked out, leave it alone.

19. If you have to pressure him into marriage, he probably doesn't want to get married. If you do, he is not the guy for you.

20. If he doesn't want to get married, don't be an underhanded bitch and trap him. This will not make you happy. In fact, this will just piss him off! Why would you want to be with someone who doesn't want you anyway?

21. Men do NOT care about things like wedding details. Give them a time, date and address to show up. That's all they want to know.

22. It's not really that they do not like fruity, alcohol drinks. It is just against the "rules" to drink one in front of people.

23. Same with straws.

24. Same idea with directions!

25. Don't ask about the "guy rules". They don't know who made them, they do not care. They make sense to them, so deal with it!

"Un" Love

Why do you invite us,
If you do not want us around?
Do you really believe that we appreciate
Standing alone in a room full of people?
We did not come here to be ignored,
So why do you bother?

Is this what you meant by moral support
And sticking together despite the circumstances?
We believed you when you told us,
That we would always be family.
That once you love someone,
You cannot "un"love them,
Just because someone else did.

Yet, here we are,
Pushed out of the circle,
Left standing out in the cold,
Watching our family as outsiders,
Though we had tried so hard to belong.

We cannot fight forever.
We will not beg you to accept us,
To know us,
To love us.
The loss is yours.
We gave you all that we had,
And not a difference was made.

If you are offended,
A side-effect of your decision,

We are terribly sorry,
But this can no longer go on.
Please make a note in your RSVP section,
That from this day forward,
To your invitations,
We must respectfully decline.

Unrealized Wish

If anyone had asked,
Only two fortnight ago,
Could I fall in love with you,
I would have answered, "No".
For you and I are just friends,
Who gave into a passing fancy,
Along the way,
And our trust in each other,
Created companionship.

How could I have been so blind?
Now I cannot imagine a world,
In which anyone could help,
But to adore you.
So sweet, so considerate,
So easy to be with.
To not love you,
Would be wasting my heart.

How odd to plan your life,
And have it not turn out as dreamt,
But to have the unexpected events,
Which throw our lives into a tailspin,
Be our greatest adventures.
That is you, to me.
The unexpected, the unplanned,
The undreamt that changed my world.

Now my answer is "yes".
I do love you!
I proclaim it loudly,

With all the strength of my being,
Without fear,
And with all my heart.
You are the dream come true,
I never realized I wished for.

What You See...

Do you like what you see?
I sure hope you do,
Because I am not changing,
And that is the honest truth.

I am comfortable in my sweats,
With no makeup and flat hair.
Most of the time I walk barefoot,
If I am cozy I do not care.

I try not to wear dresses,
Flashy jewelry or high heels.
It is all too restricting,
I do not like how it feels.

There is a time and place,
To look and act like a Lady.
That time in not at all,
When I am at home with my baby.

I have never been a girlie-girl,
Tomboy is much more my style.
I will gladly trade a skirt away,
For my jeans crumpled in a pile.

You want to know,
What there is to know about me?
Well take a good look,
Because what you get, is what you see!

World of Beauty

When I am with you,
I enter another world,
And through your eyes,
I see myself as you do...

I never understood,
What your words really meant.
Perhaps it was easier not to hear,
That someone could find so much beauty,
In one so flawed...

You once told me,
That my physical scars,
Were the marks of a great warrior,
Who has fought well in battle.

You said the lines,
That cross my breasts and belly,
Showed a Goddess, a mother,
Who loved the child that had grown inside,
Above all else.

In my haunted eyes,
A seer shows through.
One who has seen so much pain and cruelty,
Without being able to save
Those fated to the unfortunate touch.

My broken heart,
Belongs to an Angel,
Who could love more,
Than any mere mortal could receive.

You found passion, where I hid my pain.
You found a burning fire, in a cold tomb.
You found a living soul, in a lifeless body.
I found you…my light in the dark,
Where I feared no man would tread.

When I am with you,
I enter another world,
And through your eyes,
I see myself as you do…
This is the world in which I chose to be.

You

As I lie here awake,
Thinking about you,
I do know,
All my dreams have come true.

I love you,
With all my soul
And heart,
I pray our love,
Will never grow apart.

As you hold me,
In your arms
Or hold my hand,
Believe me I know,
How fortunate I am.

No matter how close
Or how far,
I know my heart,
Is where you are.

Your Oath

I made that vow,
Years ago
To love, honor and cherish.
My dear, that oath was not just for him,
But for you as well.

The bond that was our marriage,
Has broken into pieces,
But not my promise to you.
Never, my promise to you.

To love, honor and cherish,
You as my child as well.
To keep you safe,
And love you as my own.
That vow is a solid,
As the trees of the petrified wood.

Child not of my body,
But of my heart.
You are my family,
And will always remain.

You are welcome in my heart,
My home,
And my life.
I love you always!

For my beautiful and wonderful step-daughter,
Cora Lyn

Breinigsville, PA USA
24 November 2010
249957BV00002B/48/P